As the Hand,
the Glove

poems by

Pat Boran

The Dedalus Press
24 The Heath • Cypress Downs •
Dublin 6W • Ireland

www.dedaluspoetry.com

ISBN 1 901233 80 4 (paper)
ISBN 1 901233 81 2 (bound)

Acknowledgements are due to the editors and producers of the follow-
ing where a number of these poems, or versions of them, originally
appeared: *The Irish Times, Poetry Ireland Review, Fishamble Theatre
Company programmes, Café Review* (USA), *Chaffin Journal* (USA),
The 2River View (USA), *Dun Laoghaire Poetry Now anthology 2000,
The Living Stream, The Portable Creative Writing Workshop, News 2*
(Network 2), *Rattlebag* (RTE Radio 1), *Céide, Irish Writers' Centre
website and Grogan's website.* Many thanks to Theo Dorgan for advice
and feedback on the manuscript.

Cover photograph by Michael Boran

Pat Boran's website is at www.patboran.com

Dedalus Press books are represented and distributed in the
U.S.A. and Canada by **Dufour Editions Ltd.**, P.O. BOX 7,
Chester Springs, Pennsylvania 19425 and in the UK by **Central
Books**, 99 Wallis Road, London E9 5LN

Printed in Ireland by Staybro Printing Ltd., Dublin

The Dedalus Press receives financial assistance from An
Chomhairle Ealaíon / The Arts Council, Ireland

The Dedalus Press

As the Hand, the Glove

Pat Boran

Contents

for Raffaela

MILKMEN

The doorbell rings. I go.
I'm fourteen. That's how it is,
no need to stop or think.

It's the milkman's eldest son
putting a brave face on it,
wearing his father's shade.

So quietly he pours the milk,
pours its at-first thin,
then rolled, then muddy sound

until the gallon is filled.
I close the door and wait
for the milk to settle down.

Years later — for it is years
already — I begin to know
what it means, this opening

of doors, of silences, to accept
things not made on the spot
but handed over: love, inheritance.

EDEN

Sundays were where flowers blazed
in water. The sky bled
and organ music cooled like bread
in the stony light. In a kind of daze

that seemed to last forever, I went
to our two-tree orchard to catch fruit
in my open shirt, holding my breath
so I might hear the creak of the nuts

and bolts that held the world in place
and would release it. And if it was
winter or spring, if frost had put lace
finishing on the hedgerows, or if tiny paws

of new growth were pushing up through earth,
I'd take all that in too
in that between-time place where one thing at least was true,
they were blood relations, death and birth.

No Man's Land

The world began with our house.
At night if you listened hard
you could hear a whole universe
still forming. Out in the back yard

where the Milky Way stretched between
the roofs of cut-stone sheds,
bats flittered in the beams
of our flashlights, their tiny heads

like turned-out pockets. Closer,
water dripped or gushed, the dog
sensed something, cocked an ear
then stood as if the hands of a clock

had frozen somewhere. I was back
in No Man's Land again, a place
I loved, and feared, the black
damp air pressed against my face

like a hand. Behind me at the door
separating in and out,
womb and world, a dozen or more
slugs would gather, dumb, devout

as guard dogs, thick as eels
or old rope, drawn by the light
or warmth of the house, the wheels
and spirals of their journeys bright

as silver dust in honey. So when
the time came to go back, to leave
that strange land, head down I ran
as fast as I could, leaping clear

of the lair of teeming serpents, with luck
making it across the threshold
into human light again, awe-struck
by strangeness, bringing strangeness home.

HALL OF MIRRORS

'I'd like. . .' says the stranger standing before me, 'that!'
He points to something over my shoulder and waits.
It's a Travel Agency, though my father calls it The Shop,
and brochures that glisten with pictures of girls in all states

of undress, stretched on white sands or by pools,
cover the walls and counters behind me. I know
without looking round. But when I reluctantly do
(awkward teenage), it's something I've not seen before:

he's pointing to a small gold mirror containing
a fish-eye microcosm of the room we're in.
It's like the room in Van Eyck's *Arnolfini Wedding*
except, of course, I'm in V-neck and flares, and, thin

as a rake though I am, sport a Bruce Lee medallion.
It's important to face the world with an iron will.
So, to this strangely familiar stranger's reflection
I say 'Sorry, that mirror is not for sale.'

But before I can explain this is a Travel Agency,
a place you go when you want to go some place,
and not some newsagent's or hall of mirrors,
my father comes out and says, 'Good man, you're there.'

And in an instant it's just the two of us alone.
The stranger has vanished, as in Abracadabra.
It's the 1970s still, and all I know
begins with Abbey Road and ends with Abba.

TRACKS

Now my dog is dead,
paw prints in the concrete path
follow me instead.

POTION

Summer. My mother's time. A place
anything was possible — staying up
late into the evening, swapping grace
after meals for ice cream and a cup,

never a glass, of that special juice
she made from sugar, a few lemons and
some kind of powder whose arcane use
could not have been restricted to our clan

though no one I've asked among my friends
remembers their mothers in that queue
in Hipwell's chemists where mine spent
half of every Saturday, saying 'And how are you?'

to every new arrival. Which is strange.
For she added it to water and made water change.

DOORS AND WINDOWS

My father sold them, doors and windows,
entrances, exits, idyllic views
from houses not constructed yet
though mapped out with such absolute

precision that those wooden frames
we'd spend evenings stacking to the sky —
then half-days driving and unloading
in windswept fields — before our eyes

transformed. Fingers smarting
from the rasp of wood, I'd press
a fist into a palm, count to ten
and watch my breath trace silent protest

in the air, then count to ten again
while he, as I now know, in his own way —
saliva in his palm — secured the deal
and made a friend he hoped would someday pay,

though many never did. . . Then we were off,
the builders stood there, watching through the glass
that wasn't even in those windows yet, and overhead
the Milky Way already settling into place.

THE SCARECROW

was Hannigan's (Hannigan being
the one who had the brother
who went to the dance and never
came home again), standing there
west of the high thicket of briars,
arms outstretched, no hands,
a bag of air for a head, the pants
the brother left behind him in his wake,
the brother they never mentioned afterwards
for peace' sake. . .

Easy to get lost
in the endless ravelling of thoughts
that ran between all things, back then.
But back then we went, and went again,
to that top field to stare
into the absence of his face:
Hannigan's scarecrow,
in that NorthSouthEastWest
world of things half known,
an open secret.

NEIGHBOURS

They were the ones we told jokes about,
the red-necked, spud-thick family up the road:
how she smashed the car into the gate
going for her driving test, how once the door
came away in the father's hand like a sheet

of old wallpaper. And then their kid.
Helping daddy one day paint the fence
around their concrete garden, he knocked the tin
then ran away in tears, his yellow footprints
and their yellow footprints all over the street

like a dance-step map. Wee Johnny,
which is what they called him, never seemed
quite right after that. The poor wee mon, he
was frightened of his shadow. At Hallowe'en,
kids knocked on their door and threw him money

to see if he'd cry. Which he always did.
In school they ganged up on him in the yard
and made him sing *The Sash*. More than once he peed
his pants. More than once his furious dad
had to come and take him home at speed.

When the sister married, true to form
the old man drank so much he fell face first
into the wedding cake. The honeymoon,
in Ballyshannon, was a total farce.
The groom met an old flame and he was gone.

Their flat-faced dog liked to chase parked cars.
The mother opened doors in her dressing gown.
We laughed till we were sick, and then we laughed
even more. The day before they finally left town
the kid came second in a boxing match.

SUPERMARKET

Fifteen, out of the altar boys
on the grounds of age, and height, I found
my first part-time employment in
the only supermarket in town,

eating chocolate, sweeping floors,
spotting young ones, talking soccer
and always keeping the oldest
meat to the front.

On days when only one or two
roamed the aisles, it fell to me to turn
the music way down low, down slow,
so Mrs X would waltz and dream

her way past towers of toilet rolls,
would stand and stare at cans of beans
or dickied-up photos of some Fido
selling cat in chunks.

And when the place was stuffed, was packed
with dripping shoppers, little brats,
their hands like magnets, and the girls
in pencil skirts from the nearby banks,

I'd whip the tape out, that big 8-track
Strauss-filled sandwich, and lift the place
into the 20th century, volume up
as high as it went

so that Mrs X was sent skating past
Mrs Y, and their men became
trolley Jackie Stewarts, each aisle
a freeway, the whole shop a maze,

a wonder, like the streets of a town
in a film that has been speeded up
to make all the humans go tearing around
like so many ants.

But there was no film, only me
watching from the top of the office stairs
as the roll of flimsy paper crept
up and up in the cash register

manned by a girl in a navy smock,
the stenographer of all desires
and needs in that dreary,
dreaming town.

I often wondered how it felt to be
the most powerful person in that world
of haughty managers, sweet-talking reps
and foul-mouthed butchers, their hands and skirts

covered in maps of blood, until,
as if someone somewhere had pulled the plug
or called my name, the roll spun out, free,
and the whole world stopped.

FLESH

The spirit, despite bad press,
loves the flesh.

It enjoys nothing more
than body odour,

the warmth of a crotch
or the electric touch

of lips. Those dark religions
which have banned the nether regions

to the netherworld, to hell,
can cast all the spells

they like, can single out for blame
those who refuse to feel shame

about their bodies — children, the old,
the untouched inhabitants of the Third World,

but most of all those women of loose morals
whose torture is somehow part of the quarrel

about sanctity and sin
and the vessels the soul is to be found in.

Enough idols and bones!
Enough gleaming chalices and altar stones!

I say it again: the spirit loves
the flesh as the hand, the glove.

And if you doubt me, ask my dying father
which he would rather:

to be done at last with love and pain,
or to leave, but then come back to flesh again.

Am

(i.m. Nicholas Boran)

1.35 a.m.
I look at my watch and see
my life story:
I thirty-five am.

And if I press this button here
I get the date, 1999,
the year when my *am* begins to mean
something new, something else,
your *was*, your *was no longer*,
the year of your death.

The King

'The king is dead,
long live the king,'
the king thinks,
sitting, staring
at this portrait of himself,
this fresh-faced prince.

• • •

Girls with flowers' names,
the king calls them to him.
He has them sit around the hall
and slowly walks among them.
Eyes shut,
he inhales.

• • •

'Wanna see a map,' says the fool,
'of a place you've never been?'
He has the king remove his shirt
and spread it on the floor.
No one speaks. No one has to.
The king knows what this means.

THE DISAPPEARING ACT

These hands take things,
shake things, make things
disappear.

These hands, literally,
for hands are all there are
in this dark space

lit up with hope and purpose,
sharp as bright ideas
against emptiness.

One, the left,
makes the 'watch this' sign
then points to the right

and plucks a perfect flower
out of thin air
thick now with applause.

The kids go wild.
For them, this breaking of the cause
and effect chain

is a kind of dream
with evidence. Already you can see
their tiny hands repeat

the stylised moves.
Though doubts remain.
As the curtain falls

into the magician's
battered case, the birthday child
is upset, confused:

'Ma,' she wails,
'make him do it again.'
But, as Ma well knows,

there's no going back.
Life's unfair? Well, tough.
She smiles at friends,

the other single parents,
and then leans in
towards her little gem:

'Magic's not like fighting, love,'
I imagine her say. 'It's over,
not beginning, when the gloves come off.'

HAIKU

Lovers in the park,
her hands holding his hands down.
Gift of powerlessness.

CHAOS

Simple shapes are inhuman. They fail to resonate with the way nature organises itself or with the way human perception sees the world
— James Gleick

By the time I get there, the house is just a shell.
On one wall I see the marks where my father's keys
hung above the range, and opposite
a door that once led somewhere. Little else.

The kitchen has become the yard once more.
So much for expansion. And the hall,
once set with in-laid tiles, is now a sprawl
of stones and mortar. The front door

has to be propped up to hold the street
at bay. And overhead, without beams,
floors or walls, upstairs is one big room
filled with unfamiliar light.

Months from now, my father dead, we'll be back,
my mother, sisters, brothers and myself
to visit a new two-storey space
with its bland smoothness, its almost perfect lack

of character. In its one big window,
we'll line up side by side to face the street,
and have our pictures taken from the path
outside, casting ourselves as the resident ghosts.

For the moment, surrounded by the mess
of rubble, the solid walls of my childhood,
it doesn't feel as bad as I thought it would.
The worst loss is the slowly dawning loss.

MORNING

The things I see in sleep:
swans, knives, stopped clocks. . .

What some might call dreams
are for me visits to museums
of unsettled things

like myself now, in shoes and socks,
less than at home with being.

For S with AIDS

When a star dies, my love, my man,
when it gets so tired, burnt out, so heavy,
it starts to fall back into itself,
it starts to grow in density, shrink
until, at last, there comes a time
when light escapes from it no more,
when time means nothing any more,
when science, naming and love itself
wring their hands at the hospital door.
Nothingness, absence, passing, loss. . .
our secret, sleeping partners, S.

2.

Ouroboros, the mythological serpent
consuming itself, renewing itself,
the snake of Eden, snake of the tree,
the serpent coiled round the staff of being
still found on local chemists' signs,
like the one where you binged on vitamins —
what was it, three years back? — all set
to fight what you were sure was 'flu,
then toothache, backache, headache, gout. . .
Now your name cannot be spoken here
in these half-lit corridors leading nowhere
but I can hear your playful hiss,
snake brother, snake lover, S.

3.

Close up, the red-shift of apple skin
is a microcosm of the universe,
at once unbounded and finite.
See, what they did not tell us, S,
was that in Eden there were many trees
and many apples on their boughs,
on the skin of each whole galaxies,
in the core a constellation of seeds.
Unpicked the apple would still have fallen
to return to death and be born again
in whole new trees, in each apple of which
new seeds, new orchards, whole new Edens.

PS — And S, the snake's sloughed skin
is what he was, or will be, not what he is.

AFTERLIFE

(i.m. Lar Cassidy)

They're back in the back yard at it,
at it strong,
in that creaking red Escort
with the headlights left on

so they flood the room.
I've only just heard
about your death over the phone,
those few and terrible words

which the living must accept
as a new place to begin,
and I was about to do what
I've done before, fling

something, lift the window
and fling something to bring
those shaggers to their senses —
Do it all you like, sing

if you're so moved
but kill the lights. There are souls
trying to sleep (or mourn or brood)
under your jerking strobes. . .

On other nights, and, yes,
there have been months on end
since I set in here like stressed
concrete, the only godsend

the heat in these woollen folds,
on those nights
before I knew you, long before
we even met, when quiet

was the last thing I needed,
I might have got up, opened
this window to roar my delirium
or, more likely, left unspoken

the extent of my irritation
and just stood there or lain
here as I do now in the nation
of one we all become again

when the lights go out.
The time of listening.
But tonight you're dead, though not yet
out of reach — if anything

all the great teachings teach
is true — so maybe it's right
that in the light of all their fuss
out there and the darkness of my wait

in here for the day's return,
you should be rising up
on this twin helix, carried aloft
or on to where our wavering hope

in an afterlife,
in a better life and love
and place than this,
will be, if there is a god, absolved.

GRIEF

There is no consolation.
The streets of the city
are windswept, forsaken.
Broken glass
glistens on the footpath.
The train station
you've come to know so well
is deserted. Newspapers
litter the tracks, worthless
as memories. A bag
with nothing in it but a rat,
the only sign of life.

You hear
the lonely echo of your footsteps
unable to find you,
see your shadow
wind around you,
dissolve into you then
reappear behind you, as the lights
along the platforms pick you out
one by one by one, like rooms
or bright ideas you wander through
but do not recognise
the meaning of.

It's night. Keep
your eyes wide open. If you weaken
it will all be over, you'll have learned
nothing from the nightmare
yet again. If you tire or start
to drift, go splash
your face with water, stand
by the keening hand-dryer
all night long if that is what it takes
in that bruising purple light
in which the junkie
cannot hope to find the vein.

UNBUILD

I think the stairs bare.
I recall the tacks,
all three boxes we whacked
into them back there,

back then in the past, now
all for one and one for all
drawn out, withdrawn, or
the right word — recalled.

Then the stairs itself.
From the corridor of space
I remove the zigzag shelf
down which I raced,

up which I crawled
when they sent me off to bed.
And now when night falls
I go back again,

I unbuild the house.
Stone by blessed stone
I have taken it apart,
and still it is not gone.

MERRION HOUSE SESTINA

I live and work on the top floor at the back
of this four-storey building. Mostly I go
through the motions. Each morning as I watch
a gradual transformation take place
in these lanes and car parks, the light
returning to a city that seemed lost

only hours before, it's the lost
I feel drawn to, those neighbours in the back
of my mind in a house where even daylight
no longer enters. While office workers go
about their business, resuming their places
behind drawn blinds and screens, I watch

for things I can't explain to them: that swatch
of tarmac there, now matt, now glossed
with a shower of rain; the commonplace
miracle of buddleia; and here, back
from her travels above the archipelago
of rooftops, that female gull, in flight

a creature without weight until she alights
with a thud in the nest above me to watch
over her young. And though it's not so long ago
since other families grew up here, felt lost
as they waited for a parent to come back
with food, or news, with proof of other places

beyond this house, that was another place,
another time. These days there's just my light-
sleeping beloved, myself, and gulls. And at the back
of this maze of lanes, late at night, the watching,
cautious eyes of an urban fox. Do the last
secretaries suffering from the vertigo

of computer screens see her? I've seen her go
down these lanes, a shadow in a place
of shadows, a creature that has lost
one world and found another. Before the light
returns, she slips into the spaces no one watches,
no one remembers. And then I'm here, back

in the go-slow chair of poetry, the resident hunchback
of this haunted, haunting place where my wristwatch
like myself struggles out of loss and into light.

LITERATURE

His penis hanging between his legs
like a vandalised telephone, or some
deep-sea creature that cannot bear
solitude so it hangs on,

this naked man is what I am —
and yet how unlike me he seems,
surprised in this mirror I was dashing past
on my way through the house at 4 a.m.

And when a light comes on somewhere,
quick as a flash he turns away
like a man who would keep his truth concealed,
this Rosebud, this Jekyll, this Dorian Gray.

THE WHEEL

for Theo Dorgan

I found a wheel.
That is my sorrow.
It cannot sit still
and be itself.
It wants to lift, shift, roll things, be
the centre of change.

I give it change.
I take it to the theatre;
it squeaks.
I play it the most wonderful
classical music;
it lies there and groans.
I give it drink,
an obvious mistake;
it loses its former
good humour, roars
like a bull with a lance in its throat,
totals the room.

Then this afternoon,
coming home
from a match (where it leaned
like a headstone),
what did we pass?
The car plant:
cogs, rivets, those white conveyor belt
wheels by the score, wheels

like a line of gleaming Os,
in continuous surprise.
And, no surprise, the wheel
went into a spin, a whirr, a positive —
Yeats's word — gyre!
It took me everything I had
to get us both back home
and settled down. And now

it's late. Now I'm tired.
The grate has given up
the last memory of heat.
Sheets of icy rain are drawing in
from the North-West, the North-East,
and it's clear
why the Romans took one look at us out here
in Winterland
and said, no way.

The kind of night
when there's nothing better
than the promise of rest, of sleep,
of Hibernation Once Again
as they used to say;

when all I want
is just to sit like this
and listen to the sound of nothing much,

there's the wheel, the wheel
crying like a child for my touch.

WIRELESS

Was there anyone back then who didn't love
its name — the only thing on earth defined
by absence? Wire-less. That household god
looking down on us all, a coffin of sorts
until someone switched it on

and it hummed into life, hummed
even between stations the song
of origin, of background radiation.

And how it lit up
slowly then glowed like the ghost
of a hurt, like the ghost of my father
on a chair, reaching for its dial,
a safe-cracker breaking into the vaults
of sound, or breaking out into the world beyond
our sleepy, listening midland town
in a house since vanished.

2.

Here in the park, more than thirty years on,
a group of men sit and listen
to a football match. The neat beds and borders
might be the sun-dappled vines
of Marconi's own vineyard, so great

is their passion, their excitement and my own
sense of loss. To close my eyes now is to run
back through those vines, down our yard,
back past the must-smelling sheds, is to find
my father still there in the dark on that chair

staring into deep space, as if
he had known all along I'd be back,
that the message he had sent, like a voice
down invisible lines, would unite us again.

First Lesson in Alchemy

Rabbit, swan, deer, butterfly...
Out of nowhere, and with empty hands,
my father brought the shadow world to life.

Usually it happened late at night:
he'd light a candle, fix it on the stand,
then rabbits, swans, deer, that butterfly

and creatures I had never heard described
changed one into the other. Understand?
My father brought the shadow world to life.

Spelled out like this, it doesn't seem quite right,
quite true, this miracle of the midlands
where rabbits, swans, deer or even butterflies

were seldom to be seen in broad daylight
in the few square miles that confined our lives back then.
My father brought a shadow world to life?

And yet that's what he did. Before our eyes
his simple gesture made the known expand.
Rabbits, swans, deer, butterflies...
Now my father gives the shadow world new life.

Door Man

I'm a door man,
by which I mean
there is a man
and I observe him carefully,
and he is fond of doors;

as fond as JBS Haldane
imagined God must be
of beetles (why else
so many?); as fond
of night as is day;
as fond as is any kindergarten kid
of his daddy.

I'm a man
in a doorway in a Georgian street
watching the world rely
on belief in itself
to make it through the night
into the morning shift.

Lift, hold, sigh; lift...
The Spanish waitress, tanned, lithe,
from number 21, goes by on the road
to some Santiago
of the mind, goes past
this green and, strangely, gold
cave mouth, once the viewing stand
where dear old Rose and Vincent

stopped and stood,
framed in wood and brick
they didn't need to own to love,
as people do not own the past
who have been through it;

this very door
where now I stand, a man
who finds it hard to say *myself*
and mean it, for whom every I
is but another access point
to inscape, outlook.

The midwife's advice to mothers
on one side — *push* —
the undertaker's
to bell-ringing altar boys on the other,
almost any door along this street
could have been this door...

But this door,
even now in the dead of night,
turns its profile to the street,
looks out into the middle distance which
is where I step in, stop a moment
to glance back on a world
come through, and know

that just as that man right now there
across the way is also heading home —
a filthy sleeping bag across his back —
either one of us might be
what in these hard times we seem
to be, to passers by if not ourselves,
men of the world.

MACHINES

One night in York Street
almost ten years back — so much
drink and junk around the place

it was hard to say
just who was us, or them — one night
as I lay down on my own

cold slab of light, it started up:
below in the street, a car alarm
wielding its terrible, surgical blade

of sound. Across the way,
the College of Surgeons grinned in the night
like a skull, like a stack of skulls,

but it was hard not to cheer
when someone from a few doors up
suddenly appeared. A yard brush

like a weapon in his hands, he climbed
onto the gleaming bonnet where he stood
and began to swing,

first with aim and intent, so that
one by one the front lights went in, then
the indicators, windscreen wipers, the windscreen itself...

and then like some half-man, half-thing
swung, swung, swung, swung,
swung till his muscles must have ached,

till the mangled brush tumbled from his grip
and he stopped, turned, looked up at us and roared
as if his spirit could no longer be contained

by the silence, by the darkness,

by the slow-motion tragedy of
so much of Dublin back in those
and still in these dehumanising days.

HOUSEWORK

All day I have been squeezing shirts
as if they were necks. In a kind
of blind fury, I like to take it out
on things that need washing, shifting or,
if I'm lucky, smashing up. There is
perfection in a filthy bag of coal
standing in a street as cars speed past,
and something more than gravity fights back
every step of four steep flights of stairs.
And who could deny there's something just as good
as the blood of enemies or the sweat of love
in coal-dust handprints on your shirt
and a bag that might contain a corpse
inside the door? It's almost May
and not even cold, but damn, it feels
better now already. It is worth
two whole days of blisters out of seven
to see the furniture rearranged, remade,
piles of papers banished, strange space
making itself at home, as something else
finds itself at ease and settles in,
something that is without, as yet, a name,
and outside at least one man's laundry waves
its flag of surrender in the breeze.

The Washing of Feet

It's the simplest form of healing:
late at night,
the washing of feet.

When the light called sky
is an absence,
when the traffic's asleep;

when song
is a physical thing
needing physical shape

but you're just so worn out
facing darkness again
and those brave

tulips and roses
in Merrion Square
have long since turned in

to the dark, cottony
breath that simmers
inside of them.

When the world
is a cave, a dungeon,
when the angels retreat,

return to this tiny
pacific ocean,
to the washing of feet.

Turning

(i.m. Michael Hartnett)

The desk calendar on its last leaves.
In the lampshade a tiny spider weaves
a winter shroud.
The sky is a single cloud
darker still to the west
where the skull of a martin's nest
grins in the eaves.

A Box of Keys

A box the size of a small suitcase.
It was the buildings he'd misplaced.

TEARS

I like to cry
I like to cry so much
first thing I did when I was born
was cry
cry up a storm,
cry up
two small torrents
two strong currents.
The world
slapped me as a signal
to begin
so I began
as I determined to continue
with tears.

All through my childhood years
I cried, sometimes
howling my release
my relief
my glad return
to the vale of tears.
Right up until the time
the hormones came
out of hiding
out of waiting
and began
their slow tour of my body
tears
came easily.

In my teens they stopped.
My tears went underground
like the small streams
I played in as a boy
before the town grew up.
I knew they were there.
I felt their pull,
their attraction, but found
neither spring nor river mouth
where they might whisper
back to the greater
rhythm of ocean,
the ocean of tears.

No tears for instance
at seventeen
where there was more
to cry about
than I could explain,
and far too few
in recent years
when the brightest light
in the night sky
began to fade.

But now
I'm always close to tears,
at home with tears,
and not only my own but yours,

my love. I see or hear
or somehow sense
that hot swell as I cross a room,
and pass a stranger in the street
as if all eyes
were forcing me to recognise
something in the air.

And I have seen myself
in the future, prepared
to move on, move out
of the way, the room,
through doors maybe
but back to a place
where tears are rolling
down my face
as the world lifts
its hands from my flesh,
and I am lighter, light again,
and the sound of that
original slap
runs backwards before
all is quiet again,
all is still again,
and my eyes sit still
in my skull again,
only salt now, dry salt now
where once there were,
I'm glad to say,
my tears.

STILL LIFE WITH CARROTS

When I discover a carrot, like this one
grown old, forgotten on a shelf
behind bottles of oil, herbs and spices,
all those *nouveaux arrivés*, I feel myself

drawn to it. It's as if all
the wonderful meals my life has been made of,
the exotic tables at which I have sat
had never existed; as if during love-

making a former lover had come
into my mind or a neighbour, long dead
had knocked on the door and let himself in,
as of old, trailing the earth from his grave.

The politeness accosts me. Almost as frail
as my father in his hospital bed
those last long months, this carrot seems
to have something to tell me. The fact is, in the end

the formidable weakens, the once proud
become stooped and sad. The lost
no longer recognise themselves.
And so it goes for all our vegetable loves:

the pea dries up; the tomato weeps
and weeps an ectoplasmic mess;
lettuce browns like an old book;
potatoes send up flares of distress;

but carrots just age there, waiting to be found
as the plates on the table, like the planets, go around.

FALUN GONG

The young Chinese men and women
barely move at all. That's what's so strange.
You've read that in China they're outlawed,
hunted down like terrorists. Arraigned,
convicted and sentenced for crimes
against the state, many are not seen again.
Then today you take a short-cut through the park
and there they are, a small man dressed in silk
and an even smaller girl in a yellow tracksuit,
breaking all known laws: they are standing still
in the middle of rush-hour, for all the world
like two figures from a painting by Chagall,
the moment before flight, their arms outstretched,
reaching towards the limits of themselves.

VIRGIN AND CHILD ENTHRONED WITH SAINTS
after a painting by Cosimo Rosselli

The first thing that strikes you is just how ugly
both of them are, the young Virgin who looks
like a hungover hippie — the red smock,
the braids in her hair — almost laughably

bored out of her mind, her eyes half closed
as if she cannot bear it; and the kid
balanced on her knee like a small pig
that's been fattened up for slaughter. It's a pose

more likely to sell doughnuts than salvation.
You can't help wondering about Rosselli,
what he was up to, what he must have been telling
the men in power to land these commissions

others would have killed for. And sometimes did.
But maybe that helps to explain those guys
in the gilded robes and beards. Maybe that's why
they're standing around holding books and quills,

ignoring the mother, apparently deep
in conversation. 'I got this cross', the one
on the far left might be saying, 'for half nothing.
Even double the price would have been cheap.'

While another, barefoot, says: 'Like the shoes, by the way.'
And the one in the shoes stares back at his feet
and feels maybe just a pang of guilt. But at least
he can feel, he does feel, still, some days.

FILLING STATION
after a painting by Edward Hopper

The man in the filling station looks like death.
I say, 'Must get some quiet days around here.'
He doesn't even answer. Instead
he turns his back, his polyester shirt sleeves
whipping around his skinny tattooed arms.

I see him with many lovers in his past
in that big crumbling cinema over the road,
a tough guy then, a man fathers might watch
if he didn't move so fast, if he didn't know
or seem to that the boys from those small farms

back up the way were out to get him, that
given half a chance they'd stamp him out
like a cigarette dropped in a barn.
There was fire there once, of that no doubt.
Now he looks as if he's made of ash,

as if the wind could break him, or the rain
coming now in a black cloud from the north
might wash him clean away, leaving no trace
in words unless a single postcard worn
to shreds in a pocket. *Baby, I can't wait...*

THE RAISING OF LAZARUS
after a painting by Aelbert Ouwater

The kitchen was a bombsite
the night my father found the corpse
of our neighbour Paddy Walsh
spread across the floor like
a misfired human cannonball.

He called the guards. The priest arrived
and told him to take a stroll across
to Lewis's pub. A double short
seemed better than his usual pint
after that terrible shock.

An hour later, the pub full
of red-eyed mourners, who limped in
but Paddy Walsh, the man himself,
not looking bad for having gone
all week without a square meal.

THE WATCHERS
after a photograph by Ernst Haas

More than ever I wonder about them,
the unknown people who sit watching us
in small rooms somewhere surrounded by
over-flowing ashtrays, plastic cups

and walls of screens. What their names are;
their ages and sexes; what they think
when they think they're not thinking; what they see
today that they could not have seen

that first day on the job. How must it feel
to hover all day like a god
or minor angel, unable to make
the slightest difference? Unless they love

being the watchers, unless what they need
is the distance, the comfort of fiction,
it must be hell. The hours and days
must drag by in those hot-air balloons,

those diving bells. I imagine marks
on walls counting off the first kiss,
the hundred-thousandth kiss, though I guess
zooming in and out must loose its charm.

And when the shift is over, when the next
wave of angels arrives, what do they feel
stepping out into streets where they become
the strangest things on earth to the pals

watching over them now? These men
and women suddenly made flesh
and blood, hands inside gloves
and scarves wrapped around their necks

against the cold like the bandages
that give the invisible man his shape.
They must want to look up into the lens
and mouth the words: *I know you're there.*

THE VOICE ON THE JUKEBOX SANG *MAYBE...*

In a black hat and black coat,
with the kind of movements a crow makes
when it tries to tear itself away
wing by wing from hot tar,
he was there in the bar.

What happened next? Well, no one spoke
for a start; no one, I suppose,
had any words they felt might match
the 3-dimensional shock of him,
this tongue of black fire — man,

the only animal with foreknowledge
of his own imminent death.
All right, come on, joke's over,
said the barmaid in mid forward
bend that might have flashed a breast

to some old drunk... But Christ, not this,
a man stood there, held there, run through
with the current of his heart, unhid
in this one moment she would deny
that at once denies her and demands she live.

WINTER

Ice over everything out here,
the cut-stone walls,
the ruts of bikes and tractors,
ice overlaid
on comings and goings.

Even an old milker
is just a ghost of her former self,
whisper-thin
on a hill field,
the grass
crunching sadly as she goes

as if spirits had —
and sometimes what we know
is what we fear —
the weight of the real.

PONQUOGUE

"…all the lands, woods, waters, water courses, easements, prof-
its & emoluments thence arisinge what soeuer, from the place…
where the Indians hayle over their cannooes out of the North
bay to the south side of the Island, from thence to possess all the
lands lying eastward between the foresaid bounds by water…"
— Indian Deed of December 13, 1640

for Gerard Donovan

This baby shark washed up on the beach
only hours ago. The eyes, still in its head,
seem to stare into a space between worlds,
the old and new, the living and the dead.

It's the first time in America for both of us.
Out here on Long Island, buffeted by winds,
where the sun is just a white disc in the sky,
we're face to face, me about to begin

a long-promised holiday, this shark
like a symbol of all those who never made it
this far, or who did make it but found
nothing is as promised. Waves shift

and pull at his tail as if they will draw him
out again, and gulls screech overhead
waiting for us to leave so they can feed
on the soft eyes first then on the flesh.

Maybe it's just jet-lag, the fiction
of almost instant travel catching up
but something in me knows this is not my place,
this beach stretching for miles in either direction,

the land behind us once covered in oak
like the land back home. I feel as if I've stepped
through a mirror and am looking at myself
from outside now, that other, shadow realm.

2.

The road sign read Ponquogue, a Shinnecock word
meaning *the pond at the place where the bay bends.*
For all that land, the Indians received
sixteene coats, three score bushells of corne

and the promise of protection. It all sounds
so bloody familiar. And today I read
the same Indians taught the settlers how to hunt
for deer and bear, the ancient, earned techniques

of whaling from dug-out oak canoes;
how to steam open shellfish in large pots;
how to weave fishing baskets and mats
from the once abundant rushes; how the penobscot

or root of the yellow lily could be picked
and cooked with meat soup for thickening;
how to catch bass using lobster pieces
as bait; how a simple, sudden quickening

of clouds meant heavy weather up ahead,
weather that would send deer into cover.
How it is, or was at least. How the land worked
and could be worked. What a shark beached in air

or a traveller still finding his feet might glimpse
in some middle distance. What the empire stole:
the need for difference, otherness, for places
that remain beyond us even as they make us whole.

A Natural History of Armed Conflict

The wood of the yew
made the bow. And the arrow.
And the grave-side shade.

THE MELTING POT

Sick in New York, in Chinatown,
I go to a Ukranian doc
who gives me a shot in the arm and says
'Straight to bed for you, my friend.' So I book

into the nearest run-down hotel,
no curtains in the windows, stains
like maps on the mattress, a hanger stuck
in the top of the TV, half cross, half weathervane.

For the first few hours I think I'm going to die.
Bathed in sweat, I lie on my back
flicking between grainy newsreels, kung-fu
soap operas and some kind of chat

show where everyone is shouting all the time.
And then I dream, neither awake nor asleep:
a tiny Chinese man is calling out my name
from the bottom of a stairs, and up

where I am stretched out, a kid whose hands
are covered in food, in blood, leans over me until
his face is a mirror to mine, and smiles.
'Island?' he says. 'Never heard of it.'

TRANSPORTATION

The starched white sheets billowed in the wind.
It was like being on a galleon,
a hundred miles, a thousand years from shore,
hauling the line at my mother's command, setting
                                        a course for home.

WHAT'S SAVED

Save changes before closing? I click 'Yes',
thank you, computer. But I must confess

I don't remember ever stopping to think
anything like this — last carnival, first drink

and every face-flopped-into-the-pillow night
in between. Until now, the mid-year of a life

half spent on words, there hasn't been a single day
my memory's stored even one damned thing away

by asking: *Save changes before closing?*
It just does it, gets on with it, supposing,

I suppose, that exactly how things seem to be
it's how they'll stay. Lately, though, when I want to see,

when I go back to open those dustless files
from my schooldays, to flick through all those piles

of fond memories — they've been trashed! What's this?
This is not at all how I remember it!

But the fact is: when you do go back, the old country is new.
Those half-known roads no longer lead to parts of you

but to the absences of others. It's like a poem
that has lost its power by the time you get it home

into the house of words. You try to recall,
because what's saved is not what happened at all.

PENKNIFE

Still smelling of oranges
after years in this drawer
among buttons, paperclips,
envelopes, old specs...

a present from you;
designed to sever,
it's the one thing
that somehow connects.

LOST AND FOUND

Sometimes now I see my father
up in Heaven, wandering around
that strange place where he gathers up
what other souls no longer want,
as all his life he gathered
unloved things.

As if on a screen I see
his big frame bend, his bony hands
reach down for a rusted pin,
a nail, a coin from some lost kingdom.
One day it will be the very thing
someone will need.

And when the tears become too much
and this damned bed might be a field,
I sit up wondering how the hell
the world can always find more fools
to lose things and be lost themselves
and carry on.

Then something in my heart gives in,
and I know, as if I'd always known,
deep down, that all that trash, that old
Christmas wrapping, those balls of string,
the belts, belt buckles, the left-hand gloves,
the dozens of pairs of worn-out shoes
and toeless socks, the blown light bulbs,

the coils of wire and threadbare screws,
the broken clocks, the plastic bags
folded neatly, the leaking pens
and dried-up markers, the ink-stained rags
and blotting paper, the bashed-in tins
of washers, plasters, needles and lint
were never his at all, were meant
for me.

HAND SIGNALS

A winter's evening. Cycling through the rain,
fingers clenched around the handgrips,
I'm remembering those nights my hands could pass
for log rafts or the fighter planes
that dive-bombed the water in the bath,
or in shadow play could shape-shift
into rabbits, swans, deer... But times change.

People change. Determined to make them hard,
in my early teens I filled a bag with sand
and bullied it for hours. Behind the wall
of the Shaolin temple that was our back yard
I prepared for battle. Learning to fall
and rise from the dead, I'd pretend
to be first the assassin, then the bodyguard.

My hands were weapons. When they chopped air,
the air whistled. Against invisible foes
they whirled like knives. Half-inch deal
might as well have been paper, I could bear
the pain by not thinking about it. Still
my long fingers have always looked like those
strangely moon-faced figures there

steering the way. And when I stop at the lights
to flex and warm them, I hear the bones creak
and grate in my flesh. I see how my blood
after all has deserted them. So tonight,
mission accomplished, storm withstood,

I'll start over, take in reverse these streets
back to our house, our bedroom, where I'll find

you stretched out in sleep, as singular
as any unknown world. I'll rest one hand
on your warm forehead and dream once more
of a home from home, a place where all hands are
like the Famous Five, tired after adventure,
camped out in their zipped-up sleeping bags,
side by side, and gazing up at stars.

DRIVING INTO HISTORY

Once in a while, morning sunshine
filtered through the peeling paint and rust
of that old black banger perched
like a stylite up on concrete blocks

in our back garden. The seats were torn,
the wooden dashboard was an altar to insect death,
and yet my first boyhood trips into the world
were in that wheel-less, if not quite lifeless wreck.

But since they took the garden to build a bypass
to our once congested, now double-bypassed town,
I dream little of either speed or novelty
and, truth to tell, I scarcely know the names

of all these cars out here. Now all I wish

is time enough for them to age and rust,
to end up up on blocks in some child's life,
twentieth century coins down behind their seats,
their vacant windscreens open to the light.

THE ENGINE

With a four-sided aluminium key
and one hand clamped around the wheels
to hold them still, I hold my breath
and wind the engine of the small grey train.

I am five or six years old and I wind
for the soft creaking of the spring,
for the pull of these four small wheels
like the heart-throb of some living thing.

Later when I carve my name in wood
or later again stub out cigarettes
it will be with this same motion, but for now
I wind to be here, beside myself,

and with the last possible, last permissible turn
to release the perfect single ping
then watch as the engine heads out with the news,
a thing beyond me, a thing singing.